Mental Health and Self-Care for New Mothers

Table of Contents

1. Introduction 1
2. Unveiling the Complexity of Postpartum Emotions 2
    2.1. Understanding Postpartum Emotions 2
    2.2. Identifying Postpartum Emotion Triggers 3
    2.3. Dealing with Postpartum Emotions 3
    2.4. The Difference Between 'Baby Blues' and Postpartum Depression 4
    2.5. Empathy and Support: Essential Tools Towards Healing ... 4
3. Recognizing and Coping with Postnatal Depression 6
    3.1. The Basics of Postnatal Depression 6
    3.2. Understanding the Causes 7
    3.3. Treatment Options 7
    3.4. Self-Help Strategies 8
    3.5. The Role Of Supportive Relationships 8
4. The Power of Self-Care: A Guide for New Mothers 10
    4.1. The Impact of Self-Care on Mental Health 10
    4.2. Understanding Your Needs 11
    4.3. Creating a Self-Care Plan 11
    4.4. Building a Strong Support System 11
    4.5. Tackling Mom Guilt 12
    4.6. Conclusion 12
5. Incorporating Mindfulness into Your New Routine 13
    5.1. Practical Ways to Incorporate Mindfulness 13
    5.2. Mindfulness With Your Baby 14
    5.3. Mindful Motherhood Activities 14
    5.4. Mindfulness During Overwhelming Times 14
    5.5. Practicing Mindful Meditation 15
    5.6. Conclusion 15

- 6. Building a Support Network: You Are Not Alone ... 16
  - 6.1. Why Build a Support Network ... 16
  - 6.2. Identifying Your Potential Support Network ... 16
  - 6.3. Structuring The Support Network ... 17
  - 6.4. Nurturing Your Support Network ... 18
  - 6.5. Support Network Challenges ... 18
- 7. Sleep Deprivation: Strategies for Better Rest ... 20
  - 7.1. The Impact of Sleep Deprivation ... 20
  - 7.2. Understanding Newborn Sleep Pattern ... 20
  - 7.3. Practical Strategies for Better Rest ... 21
  - 7.4. Eating Right for Better Sleep ... 22
  - 7.5. Mindfulness and Relaxation Techniques ... 22
- 8. Reviving Your Physical Health After Childbirth ... 23
  - 8.1. Postpartum Body Changes ... 23
  - 8.2. Nutrition and Hydration ... 24
  - 8.3. Regaining Physical Strength ... 24
  - 8.4. Breast Care ... 24
  - 8.5. Rest and Sleep ... 25
  - 8.6. Handling Aches and Pains ... 25
  - 8.7. Seeking Medical Checkups ... 25
- 9. Balancing Motherhood and Personal Identity ... 27
  - 9.1. Acknowledging the Challenge ... 27
  - 9.2. Redefine Your Identity ... 27
  - 9.3. Self Care: A Non negotiable Aspect ... 28
  - 9.4. Practicing Mindfulness ... 28
  - 9.5. Seek Professional Support ... 28
  - 9.6. Reconnect with Your Community ... 28
  - 9.7. The Importance of Conversation ... 29
  - 9.8. Navigating Partnership ... 29
  - 9.9. Carving Out "Me" Time ... 29

10. Nutrition: Fuelling the Body, Boosting the Mind ... 31
    10.1. The Link between Nutrition, Body, and Mind ... 31
    10.2. The Fundamentals of Nutrition for New Mothers ... 31
    10.3. Essential Nutrients and their Sources ... 32
    10.4. Nourishing Your Mind: Foods that Enhance Mood ... 33
    10.5. Maiden Voyage into Mindful Eating ... 33
    10.6. Meeting Your Nutritional Needs: A Sample Meal Plan ... 34
11. Seeking Professional Help: When and Why ... 36
    11.1. Identifying the Need ... 36
    11.2. Exploring the Options ... 37
    11.3. Choosing the Right Professional ... 37
    11.4. Preparing for the First Session ... 38
    11.5. Embracing the Process ... 38
    11.6. Remember, You're Not Alone ... 38

Chapter 1. Introduction

Embracing motherhood is an exquisite journey, filled with profound love, endless delight, and unique challenges. Navigating the maelstrom of emotions and the transformative element known as 'new motherhood' is no easy feat—especially when it comes to mental health and self-care. That's precisely what our special report revolves around: "Mental Health and Self-Care for New Mothers." Through this enlightening and heartening guide, we delve into the essential strategies, practical advice, and expert insights to help new mothers maneuver this beautiful phase of life with optimum mental wellness. With a sprinkle of relatable anecdotes, a dash of scientific facts, and plenty of encouraging words, this report is your go-to compendium to foster self-care and maintain balance while embarking on the motherhood journey. Let's not forget, a happier you means a happier baby!

Chapter 2. Unveiling the Complexity of Postpartum Emotions

For a new mother, the birth of a baby brings overwhelming joy but also a plethora of emotions. These can range from intense happiness to profound anxiety and even bouts of sadness. Often unspoken about, such a turmoil of feelings is colloquially known as 'baby blues' or more clinically - postpartum emotions.

2.1. Understanding Postpartum Emotions

Postpartum emotions can be a challenging stage for a new mother, intruding upon what is supposed to be one of the happiest times of her life. This period often brings forth a mix of conflicting feelings which might include euphoria, fear, anxiety, sadness, irritability, and fatigue. Nail it down to hormonal fluctuations, sleep deprivation, or the overwhelming sense of responsibility that accompanies a new baby; it's an emotional roller coaster that very few can brace for.

Scientifically speaking, postpartum hormonal drop is rather significant and it's one of the largest hormone shifts a woman's body will experience. Within 48 hours of childbirth, hormones like estrogen and progesterone drop precipitously back to pre-pregnancy levels. This change affects the brain's production of serotonin– a neurotransmitter that helps regulate mood - causing mood swings and other associated symptoms.

2.2. Identifying Postpartum Emotion Triggers

Postpartum feelings might arise from numerous facets. Amongst them include:

- Exhaustion from labor and delivery, coupled with lack of sleep
- Overwhelm from the constant baby care
- Lack of personal time and feeling of lost identity
- Anxiety over baby's health or capability as a mother
- Body changes leading to low self-esteem
- Disconnection from your partner

Observing what can potentially stimulate these feelings may be the first stepping-stone towards coping with them.

2.3. Dealing with Postpartum Emotions

Dealing with postpartum emotions effectively involves several aspects. Here are some key strategies:

- **Rest:** Although it might be challenging amidst newborn care, catching up on sleep could drastically improve mood disorders.
- **Nourishment:** Consuming nutrient-rich foods can influence the production of mood-regulating neurotransmitters positively.
- **Sharing feelings:** Opening up about your experiences and feelings with fellow mothers, a partner, or a friend can provide much-needed relief.
- **Time out:** Making some time for yourself, even if it's just a short walk or a cup of tea, can help rejuvenate you.

- **Professional help:** If the emotions become overpowering or lead to depression, seeking professional help is recommended.

These strategies may forge a path of improved mental health and ensure the initial transformation into motherhood is smooth and pleasurable.

2.4. The Difference Between 'Baby Blues' and Postpartum Depression

'Baby blues,' the mild depression that many women experience after giving birth, is normal and typically fades within a few weeks. It's characterized by mood swings, crying spells, anxiety, and difficulty sleeping. However, postpartum depression (PPD) is more severe and long-lasting. It can include excessive crying, overwhelming fatigue, severe mood swings, and even thoughts of harming oneself or the baby. If the signs persist or escalate, seeking immediate medical assistance is crucial.

2.5. Empathy and Support: Essential Tools Towards Healing

Empathy, understanding, and support from partners, family, and friends are invaluable during the postpartum period. Emotional reassurance, physical help, or simply listening goes a long way in healing the turmoil of postpartum emotions. Encouraging the new mother to express her feelings and validating them might act as a balm to her fluctuating emotions. Remember, this is not a battle she has to fight alone.

In conclusion, postpartum emotions paint a picture that is far from the rosy scenarios social and mainstream media often depict. It is a complex phase accompanied by a host of such intense emotions that it can upend a new mother's world. Recognizing, understanding, and dealing with them is therefore essential. The postpartum period is not just about caring for the newborn but also about ensuring the mental wellbeing of the mother. Because a mother who is mentally healthy and happy can indeed foster a healthy and content baby.

Chapter 3. Recognizing and Coping with Postnatal Depression

Postpartum depression, or more broadly, postnatal depression (PND), is a serious mental health condition that can affect a woman shortly before or soon after childbirth. It is important to recognize the symptoms of this condition and understand that it is perfectly normal and okay to seek help.

3.1. The Basics of Postnatal Depression

About one in seven women experience postnatal depression. It is a common condition that can happen anytime within the first year of giving birth. Some women feel its effects immediately after delivery while others may not experience symptoms until several months later. The condition is characterized by feelings of sadness that go beyond the 'baby blues' - a milder form of mood swings and anxiety that many women experience after childbirth.

Symptoms of postnatal depression include a persistent feeling of sadness, lack of interest in the world around you, frequent crying episodes, feelings of hopelessness and low self-esteem, fatigue, sleep disturbances, and inability to bond with your baby. Severe symptoms may also include thoughts about harming oneself or the baby.

If you identify with these symptoms, remember that there is no reason to be ashamed. Understand that postnatal depression is not a sign of weakness or failure. It is simply a complication of giving birth that can be treated effectively.

3.2. Understanding the Causes

So, what causes postnatal depression? There's no single answer. It likely results from a combination of physical and emotional factors. After childbirth, the level of hormones (estrogen and progesterone) in your body quickly drop. This leads to chemical changes in your brain that may trigger mood swings. Additionally, many mothers are unable to get the rest they need to fully recover from giving birth. Constant sleep deprivation can lead to physical discomfort and exhaustion, which can contribute to the symptoms of postnatal depression.

Furthermore, the social and psychological changes associated with having a baby create an increased strain on mental health. This huge change in your life can be both joyous and stressful, and all these emotions can sometimes result in depression.

3.3. Treatment Options

Postnatal depression can be a debilitating condition, but the good news is it's entirely treatable through a variety of methods. Medical treatments, psychological therapy, self-help techniques, and support from others all play a crucial role in recovery.

In terms of medical treatments, your healthcare provider might suggest antidepressants or hormone therapy. Antidepressants can be effective in treating postnatal depression, and several types are safe to use while breastfeeding. If your depression is linked to a drop in your estrogen levels, hormone therapy might be recommended.

Apart from medication, cognitive behavioral therapy (CBT) and interpersonal therapy (IPT) are psychological therapies that have been shown to be very helpful for sufferers of PND. CBT helps you manage your problems by changing the way you think and behave. On the other hand, IPT focuses on problems in personal relationships and the personal role changes that come with being a new mother.

3.4. Self-Help Strategies

There are several self-help strategies that you can incorporate into your daily routine to help manage the symptoms of postnatal depression. Firstly, don't be too hard on yourself. Understand that being a mother is challenging and it's okay to have bad days. Try to get as much rest as you can. Sleep deprivation can make depression worse.

Eat a healthy diet to maintain your energy levels. If you find it hard to cook, consider meal planning or asking a family member to help out. Regular physical activity can also be an effective way to combat depression. Even a short walk around the block with your baby can help improve your mood.

Socialize with family and friends and join support groups as these avenues provide outlets to express your thoughts and feelings. You might find comfort in learning that other mothers are experiencing the same feelings you are.

3.5. The Role Of Supportive Relationships

Supportive relationships, including ones with a spouse, family members, friends, or other new mothers, can be particularly beneficial. Speaking with someone who can offer an empathetic ear and practical solutions, or who shares similar experiences, can help you navigate postnatal depression.

Remember, you are not alone. Many mothers face the same challenges and go through similar experiences. Finding community in these relationships can help you remember that. Sharing feelings with others can also help lessen the burden of postnatal depression.

A spouse or partner can also provide useful support, both emotional and practical. Taking turns to care for the baby, sharing household responsibilities, and just being there to provide emotional support can significantly improve a mother's mental health. And for those mothers who are single, tapping into a network of family and friends can be essential. Their support can free up time for self-care, which is crucial in managing postnatal depression.

In conclusion, postnatal depression can be a heavy burden to bear. But by understanding its causes, recognizing its symptoms, and seeking help, you can manage this condition. With appropriate treatment, self-help strategies, and support, you will overcome the challenges posed by postnatal depression and successfully embark on the beautiful and rewarding journey of motherhood.

Chapter 4. The Power of Self-Care: A Guide for New Mothers

Motherhood is an enthralling journey that comes with both immense joy and unavoidable stress. It's a transformative experience, reshaping your life in ways too multitudinous to count. Amid the whirlwind of nappy changes, midnight feedings, and lullabies, it's essential for new mothers to prioritize their mental wellbeing and self-care.

4.1. The Impact of Self-Care on Mental Health

A mother's mental health has a profound impact on her ability to care for her child, upon her relationship with the baby, and upon the baby's own development. Numerous studies have conclusively shown the link between a new mother's mental state and the baby's mood, behavior, and overall development. This crucial fact makes it imperative for new moms to prioritize their mental health.

Self-care, often defined as a series of actions and habits that help maintain physical, mental, and emotional health, is more than just an indulgence. It's a vital process that helps ward off stress, exhaustion, and mental health disorders like postpartum depression. Establishing a self-care routine can help new moms navigate the exhausting first few months of motherhood while ensuring they're mentally and emotionally fit to nurture their little one.

4.2. Understanding Your Needs

One unique aspect of self-care is that it looks different for everyone. Some may find solace in a hot bath after a long day, while others might crave a few minutes of quiet reading. The key is to identify activities that uplift you and make you feel recharged.

As a new mother, you might find it difficult to identify your self-care needs amidst the plethora of responsibilities. However, taking that time to introspect is incredibly important and can ultimately make you a better mom. Dedicate some time to reflect on your wellbeing and what your needs are—physically, emotionally, and mentally.

4.3. Creating a Self-Care Plan

The basis of a good self-care routine is a well-thought-out, realistic plan. Start by jotting down any activities or behaviors that bring you joy or solace. These can be as mundane as drinking a hot cup of tea, reading a book, meditating, or taking a short walk outdoors.

Assign time for these activities in your daily routine, ensuring it's flexible and considerate of your responsibilities as a new mom. Another important thing is to remember that it's okay if the routine doesn't come together immediately or if you need to tweak it as you go along. Motherhood is all about learning and adapting, after all.

4.4. Building a Strong Support System

Remember, self-care doesn't mean you have to do everything alone. Building a strong support system can play a significant role in easing your transition into motherhood. A network of supportive family members, friends, or fellow mothers can give you little breaks to rest, recharge, and practice self-care.

Professional support can also be worthwhile. This can include mental health experts, lactation consultants, or postpartum doulas. These professionals can provide practical advice, emotional support, and expert insights to help you better cope with the pressures of being a new mother.

4.5. Tackling Mom Guilt

A common obstacle many new mothers face in practicing self-care is the feeling of guilt. You might feel like any moment spent on yourself is a moment taken away from your baby. However, it's important to recognize that by caring for yourself, you're subsequently better equipped to care for your baby. Just as you wouldn't let your baby go without feeding, don't neglect to nourish yourself with the self-care you need.

4.6. Conclusion

Motherhood, while undeniably fulfilling, can often prove to be an emotional rollercoaster. Practicing self-care as a new mother is not an act of selfishness—it's an essential part of keeping yourself mentally healthy and thereby being better able to raise your baby. Remember, a happier, healthier you will inevitably result in a happier, healthier baby. Embrace the power of self-care to navigate the beautiful, challenging journey of motherhood with grace and positivity.

Chapter 5. Incorporating Mindfulness into Your New Routine

The transition to becoming a new mother is coupled with a whirlwind of change, both physically and emotionally—often highlighting the importance of self-care. A beneficial and powerful instrument in your self-care toolkit can be the practice of mindfulness, which can be incorporated into your new routine.

Mindfulness is the practice of focusing one's attention on the present moment, accepting it without judgment. This process allows new mothers to stay present and engaged with their babies, reduces stress levels, and improves mental health.

5.1. Practical Ways to Incorporate Mindfulness

Conscious Breath: Conscious breathing is one of the simplest ways to practice mindfulness. Noticing the natural rhythm of your breath, the sensation of air entering and leaving your nostrils, the rise and fall of your chest as you breathe can all anchor you in the present moment. This can be done while feeding your baby, putting them to sleep, or during quiet moments throughout your day.

Mindful Eating: Mothers often forget to take care of their nutritional needs amidst the baby care chaos. Mindful eating involves focusing on the sight, smell, and taste of the food, connecting you with the act of nourishment.

5.2. Mindfulness With Your Baby

Skin to Skin Contact: Spending quality time through skin to skin contact with your baby helps you pay attention to the present moment. The warmth, scent, and the physical bond with your baby can help bring your focus to the here and now.

Baby's Breath: Listen to your baby's breathing patterns. It's rhythmic, pure, and calming—a mesmerizing lullaby for you. Syncing your breath with that of your baby can be a soothing mindfulness exercise.

5.3. Mindful Motherhood Activities

Journaling: Writing down your thoughts can be therapeutic. A mindful journal can include a playful recounting of your baby's everyday actions, your worries, emotions, and feelings of gratefulness.

Morning and Night-Time Rituals: In your morning or evening rituals, incorporate mindfulness. Be it brushing your teeth or your skincare routine, acknowledge the sensations and perform the act slowly.

Aware-Walks: Taking your baby for a stroll can be a mindful act. You can engage your senses by noticing the sounds, smells, and colors around you while pushing the baby stroller.

5.4. Mindfulness During Overwhelming Times

Managing Difficult Emotions: Being a new mother can evoke a spectrum of emotions. Mindfulness can act as an emotional flotation device, helping you recognize these swirling emotions without letting them overpower you.

Breathing Exercises: When you feel your anxiety levels rising, try the 4-7-8 breathing technique. Inhale for 4 seconds, hold your breath for 7 seconds, and exhale for 8 seconds. This simple technique can help bring immediate calm.

5.5. Practicing Mindful Meditation

Meditation App: Several meditation apps offer guided mindfulness meditations specifically designed for new mothers, supporting you to find calm and balance amidst the new-motherhood chaos.

Chair Yoga: With simple stretching and breathing exercises, chair yoga can offer a mindful respite for mothers who are looking to ease physical discomfort and mental stress.

5.6. Conclusion

While the above practices are valuable ways to incorporate mindfulness into your new routine, remember it's essential not to judge your dwindling attention or feel guilty. Consistency is key, and even if you allocate a few minutes, it will weave in a significant impact. Mindful motherhood doesn't mean being a 'perfect' mother—it means being present, genuinely available to your baby, and most importantly, to yourself. Take one day at a time, one breath at a time. A mindful mother reaps benefits not only for herself but also nurtures a happier, calmer, and more peaceful environment for her baby.

Chapter 6. Building a Support Network: You Are Not Alone

In the initial days of becoming a mother, you might feel a barrage of emotions. Some mothers feel invincible, while others may feel overwhelmed. Whichever end of the spectrum you find yourself on, know this: You are not alone. Building a support network will play a crucial role during this transformative period in your life. This comprehensive guide will walk you through the process, step-by-step.

6.1. Why Build a Support Network

A support network is integral to your mental health as it provides various forms of assistance, be it emotional, physical, or informational. It offers a safety net in times of crisis, acting as a buffer against incidents of life stress and fostering a sense of belonging and security.

When navigating new motherhood, contemporary pressures and traditional societal expectations can pile up fast, making this stage stressful and daunting. A strong, reliable support network imparts reassurance, reduces feelings of isolation, aids stress management, and contributes to overall well-being.

6.2. Identifying Your Potential Support Network

Your prospective support network broadly encapsulates anyone around you who can offer help, emotional succor, or practical advice. This network could include your spouse or partner, family members, friends, neighbors, healthcare professionals, or even online communities.

1. Family, Friends & Neighbors: Their presence can be comforting, their experiences enlightening, and their willingness to share domestic chores invaluable.
2. Medical Professionals: A trusted healthcare provider can offer much-needed reassurances about your health and your baby's well-being.
3. Online Communities: Postpartum support groups on social media are brimming with mothers sharing similar experiences. Online forums and health websites can also provide useful tips and guidance.

Remember, building a network is not a numbers game. It's about including individuals who make you feel understood, respected, and cared for.

6.3. Structuring The Support Network

The most effective networks aren't built overnight. Being reflective about your needs and being proactive in seeking assistance is key.

1. Open Communication: It's essential to express how you're feeling, articulate your needs and share your concerns. People aren't mind-readers and they might appreciate your guidance about how best they can support you.
2. Accepting Help: Societal expectations often make mothers believe they have to 'do it all.' This is not only unrealistic but unhealthy. Accept assistance with gratitude and without guilt.
3. Planning Ahead: Discuss the kind of support you'll need in advance, if possible. This could involve who'll help with diaper changes, cooking, or addressing late-night baby emergencies.
4. Remember Self-Care: Factor in time for your well-being. Exercise, nutrition, sleep, relaxation, hobbies—all should be part of your

self-care repertoire. Your network can support you here by permitting you some 'me-time.'

5. Set Boundaries: The network need not always be at your doorstep; it's okay to want and ask for privacy.

6.4. Nurturing Your Support Network

Building your network requires work. Like a garden, it thrives with attention and wilts with neglect. Nurturing your network entails:

1. Appreciation: Show gratitude towards your network; thank them for their assistance regularly.
2. Reciprocity: Help should be a two-way street; be there for your network when they need you.
3. Regular Communication: Keep your network updated about your journey; sharing can deepen your relationships.

6.5. Support Network Challenges

Not everyone has access to an extensive social network. If you're new to a place, or if relatives live far away, it can be tough. Furthermore, COVID-19 has made physically connecting with people increasingly challenging. However, telecommunication, virtual support groups, and online counseling have made it possible to build and maintain a support network remotely.

In conclusion, building a support network is crucial and it should be a priority. You're not alone in your journey, and that's why building a robust support system is so essential. The steps and strategies outlined herein will help pave the way for a healthier and happier motherhood. Remember, reaching out is not an admission of weakness, but a testament to your strength and your love for your baby.

Chapter 7. Sleep Deprivation: Strategies for Better Rest

Motherhood brings many joys, but it also has its share of challenges. One of the most pervasive being sleep deprivation. With a newborn in the picture, your sleep cycle gets disrupted, leading to a host of potential issues. Lack of sleep can lead to depression, anxiety, and an overall decline in health. In this context, appropriate strategies can ensure better rest and improved overall wellbeing.

7.1. The Impact of Sleep Deprivation

Sleep deprivation can significantly affect both the physical and mental health of new mothers, impacting their ability to care for their newborn without experiencing overwhelming distress. Lack of sleep often leads to a decrease in alertness and attention span, caused in part by a reduced ability to concentrate. The immediate effects are invariably irritability, mood swings, and heightened emotional sensitivity.

According to a scientific study published in the Journal of Sleep Research, prolonged sleep deprivation can even alter the metabolism and endocrine function, leading to an increased appetite and potential weight gain. Lack of sleep can also adversely affect the body's ability to heal and strengthen its immune system, increasing the risk of infections and illnesses.

7.2. Understanding Newborn Sleep Pattern

Getting to know your newborn's sleep pattern can be instrumental in helping you devise a strategy for better rest. Most newborns sleep for about 16 to 17 hours a day. However, this sleep is often in 3- to 4-hour intervals throughout the day and night.

Your newborn's sleep-wake cycle, or circadian rhythm, is not yet developed. Typically, babies start sleeping more at night around three months of age. Until then, it's crucial to remember that your baby's irregular sleeping schedule is not a reflection of your parenting.

7.3. Practical Strategies for Better Rest

It's unrealistic to expect a full eight hours of uninterrupted sleep when caring for a newborn. However, this doesn't mean that new mothers should accept constant exhaustion. Here are a few practical strategies that can help ensure better rest:

- Establish a routine: A bedtime routine can help signal to your body that it's time to sleep. This routine could include activities like dimming the lights, turning off electronic devices, reading a book or even practicing relaxation exercises.

- Nap when your baby naps: While this can be difficult, especially for mothers who are trying to catch up on housework or tend to other children, even a short nap can dramatically improve your mood and energy levels.

- Delegate and share responsibilities: New mothers often feel the pressure to do it all. But remember, it is okay to ask your partner, family, or friends for help. You could consider delegating duties such as bottle feeding the baby at night or changing diapers to others. This can allow you to get some much-needed rest.

- Consider co-sleeping or room sharing: The American Academy of Pediatrics suggests that room sharing (baby sleeps in the same room but on a separate surface) can make nighttime feeding easier and lessen the impact on your sleep. If you consider co-sleeping (baby sleeps on the same surface), ensure it's done safely.

- Consult a healthcare professional: If, despite trying these strategies, sleep deprivation starts affecting your mental health or quality of life, consult a healthcare professional. They may guide you towards effective solutions, and evaluate whether you might be dealing with postpartum depression or anxiety.

7.4. Eating Right for Better Sleep

Believe it or not, your diet can impact how well you sleep. For example, consuming caffeine and sugar can make it harder for your body to relax. Instead, try eating more protein, high-fiber foods, and fruits and vegetables, and staying hydrated. These contain natural sugars that will help regulate your energy and can give you the stamina you need.

7.5. Mindfulness and Relaxation Techniques

Incorporating mindfulness and relaxation techniques into your pre-bedtime routine is another effective strategy. Breathing exercises, progressive muscle relaxation, or meditation can guide your body into a more calm and peaceful state, making it easier for you to fall asleep. They can also act as a kind of reset button following a demanding day.

In conclusion, while the presence of a newborn inevitably disrupts sleeping patterns, there are numerous strategies and measures to counteract these effects. Remember, self-care is not selfish; it is an essential part of being a happy and healthy mother. Your wellbeing is equally important and integral to the wellbeing and growth of your child. Always seek help if you feel overwhelmed, and remember, you are not alone in this journey.

Chapter 8. Reviving Your Physical Health After Childbirth

Physical health after childbirth is crucial, not just for the recuperation of the mother but to care for the newborn as well. The transformative journey that women embark on during pregnancy doesn't end at childbirth. A significant part of that journey lies in the recovery and rejuvenation post-delivery. This process is as physical as it is physiological and emotional. It takes tenacity, patience, as well as proper care and tips to return to optimal health and navigate this new chapter of life effectively.

8.1. Postpartum Body Changes

The journey towards renewed physical health begins by understanding the postpartum body changes. Childbirth brings about dramatic changes in your body—from hormonal shifts to physical alterations. For instance, you might experience 'afterpains,' which are contractions as your uterus returns to its pre-pregnancy size. Breast engorgement as milk production starts can also be quite uncomfortable. Other common post-delivery effects include lochia (post-birth bleeding), tender perineum especially after a vaginal birth, constipation, and hemorrhoids.

Dealing with these changes requires patience and appropriate care. Over-the-counter medication can help manage afterpains and it is safe even when breastfeeding. Warm showers and cold compresses can effectively alleviate breast engorgement. If you're dealing with constipation, a high-fiber diet coupled with plenty of fluids can work miracles. Above all, it's crucial to rest as much as possible to allow your body to heal.

8.2. Nutrition and Hydration

Proper nutrition and hydration are essential for recovery after childbirth. Your body needs a variety of nutrients to rebuild strength and repair tissues affected during delivery. A balanced diet rich in fruits, vegetables, lean proteins, whole grains, and dairy can provide those much-needed nutrients. If you are breastfeeding, your caloric needs will increase, so ensure you are eating enough.

Hydration is equally important. Drinking plenty of water enables good breast milk production and aids in your overall recovery by helping replace fluids lost during childbirth. Water, milk, fruit juices, and decaffeinated teas are excellent choices for keeping hydrated.

8.3. Regaining Physical Strength

Resume physical activity slowly and gently after childbirth. Light exercises can kickstart your journey towards getting back in shape. Remember to consult your healthcare provider before beginning any fitness regime, especially if you've had a C-section or complicated delivery. High-intensity workouts should be avoided until after your six-week postpartum checkup or until your doctor gives the all-clear.

Start with gentle walks, pelvic floor exercises, and light stretching. These activities can help ease aches and pains, boost mood, and promote better sleep. Furthermore, they set a foundation for more vigorous activities once you're ready.

8.4. Breast Care

Breast care is an essential part of your post-childbirth physical health, whether you're breastfeeding or not. Breast engorgement, cracked nipples, and mastitis are common concerns for new mothers. To prevent or ease these issues, ensure that your baby latches correctly during nursing. Regularly changing nursing pads can keep the area dry and less susceptible to infection. Lanolin cream can alleviate soreness and cracking. If any discomfort or signs of mastitis arise, promptly reach out to a healthcare provider.

8.5. Rest and Sleep

While taking care of your newborn, remember to rest and sleep as much as you can. Lack of sleep can delay your recovery, compromise your immune system, and lead to mood disorders.

Working out a sleeping schedule with your partner or a trusted family member could allow you to get more rest. Also, napping while your baby sleeps can be a great way to catch up on lost nighttime sleep.

8.6. Handling Aches and Pains

Pains, specifically backache and pelvic pain, can be a constant companion in the postpartum period. Gentle exercises and appropriate positioning while nursing can help decrease discomfort. Warm baths and heating pads can also offer some relief. Above all, listen to your body and avoid over-exerting yourself.

8.7. Seeking Medical Checkups

Regular medical checkups are vital during the postpartum period. Doctors look out for signs of postpartum complications such as infection, uncontrolled bleeding, and postpartum depression. These visits are also an excellent opportunity to discuss any concerns about your recovery and get personalized guidance.

Becoming a new mother is a rewarding but challenging voyage. Understanding and caring for your physical health is just as important as nurturing your newborn. By employing these strategies and nurturing patience and perseverance, you can progressively work towards reclaiming your health after childbirth. Remember, ensuring your wellbeing isn't only beneficial to you but your newborn as well. Happy parenting!

Chapter 9. Balancing Motherhood and Personal Identity

Motherhood invariably brings seismic changes to life. As exhilarating as it is to behold the marvel of life you've brought into existence, the gravitational pull towards your child might leave you with a disrupted sense of personal identity. Frequently, new mothers find themselves entangled within a new identity that revolves solely around motherhood, leading to feelings of invisibility and loss of individuality. However, maintaining a balance between motherhood and your personal identity doesn't imply an uncompromising tug of war; instead, it can be seen as a harmonious blend.

9.1. Acknowledging the Challenge

Acceptance is, in many ways, the first step towards balance. Embrace the fact that no two mothers' experiences are identical. Your journey is unique, and it's perfectly natural to confront trials, errors, and evolving emotions along this path. Do not succumb to the often-unrealistic standards society may impose. Postpartum period can be a challenging time for an existential crisis, as the identity shift happens almost overnight. Acknowledge these feelings, and remember, this crisis is a natural reaction to the enormous life change you are navigating.

9.2. Redefine Your Identity

Who you are is not only defined by your role as a mother but by a multitude of roles and passions that bring you joy, fulfillment, and a sense of accomplishment. You are an individual apart from being a mother—a friend, a professional, a wife, a hobbyist—the list is endless. These roles are still within you, waiting to be expressed or developed.

9.3. Self Care: A Non negotiable Aspect

Self-care should enhance your mental and physical wellbeing and should be a part of your daily routine. Exercise, nutritious meals, regular check-ups, ample sleep, and moments of solitude can invigorate your body and mind, equipping you to better welcome the joy and frustration motherhood encapsulates. Remember, it's not selfish to take care of yourself, rather essential.

9.4. Practicing Mindfulness

Staying present and focused on the moment can remarkably increase happiness and reduce stress. This can be achieved by cultivating a practice of mindfulness. Start small by focusing on your breath or indulging in activities that require your conscious attention.

9.5. Seek Professional Support

There's no shame in seeking professional help from mental health experts. Speaking with a counselor or a therapist can provide insightful guidance and tools to cope with the guilt, anxiety, or depression that may crop up due to identity loss.

9.6. Reconnect with Your Community

Don't hesitate to build or reconnect with your community. Join local mom groups, book clubs, fitness clubs, or any platform that interests you. A strong network not only gives emotional support but also serves as a reminder that you are not alone in your journey.

Remember, balancing motherhood with personal identity is a dynamic process. Each phase poses unique challenges and requires patience, resilience, and flexibility. Take baby steps and make those consistent. It's this pursuit of balance that will subsequently lead to a more content, rounded, and happier you, and indeed, a happier baby!

9.7. The Importance of Conversation

Crucially, start open conversations about postpartum experiences. Convey your feelings of identity loss to your partner, family, or friends. The more we normalize these conversations, the more we will empower each other.

9.8. Navigating Partnership

Partnerships play a significant role in this journey. If you're in one, open communication about household responsibilities and childcare can alleviate undue pressure on you. They should understand and respect your necessity for personal time and space. Achieving an equitable distribution of chores can remarkably improve your quality of life and self-satisfaction.

9.9. Carving Out "Me" Time

Creating personal space and allocating "me" time should be a priority. Spend time doing what you enjoyed pre-motherhood—be it reading, painting, writing, or just relaxing. Small breaks can have a considerable impact on your mental wellbeing and self-image.

Motherhood is indeed a demanding role, but always remember you are not merely a "mother." You are a multi-dimensional personality with various roles beyond motherhood. Hold on to your uniqueness. You're cherished as a mother, as well as an individual with wants, passions, aspirations, and dreams. There's no rush to find the balance all at once; the joy of motherhood is meant to be savoured slowly, just like the gradual and beautiful unveiling of every aspect of your evolved identity.

Chapter 10. Nutrition: Fuelling the Body, Boosting the Mind

There's a saying among health-conscious individuals — "You are what you eat." This aphorism holds significant merit, particularly for new mothers. Your body not only acts as a vessel that nourishes your newborn, but it must simultaneously recover from the strenuous journey of pregnancy and childbirth. So, it becomes indispensable to understand the connection between nutrition, your body, and mind, and bridge the gap wherever necessary.

10.1. The Link between Nutrition, Body, and Mind

Experts often highlight that mental health is not just about the mind, but the body too. Postpartum depression, anxiety, or simply overwhelming stress — these are real challenges for new mothers and profoundly affect mental wellbeing. Here's where nutrition comes to the rescue. A diet comprising the right nutrients can fuel your body correctly and help uplift your mood. Whole grains, lean proteins, fruits, and vegetables stimulate the production of serotonin (a neurotransmitter linked with good mood), all while nourishing the body.

10.2. The Fundamentals of Nutrition for New Mothers

A balanced diet for new mothers is built upon certain nutritional fundamentals.

- Carbohydrates: Opt for complex carbohydrates found in whole grains and vegetables. They help with satiety and energy.
- Proteins: Proteins are the building blocks of your body tissues and ensure your body's recovery post-delivery.
- Fats: Healthy fats like Omega-3 fatty acids are crucial for brain health, and promote hormonal balance.
- Vitamins and Minerals: A variety of vitamins like A, C, D, E, K, and B-complex, along with minerals like Iron, Calcium, Magnesium, amongst others, contribute to overall health and wellbeing.

Remember — your body has different needs now, and simply reducing meal sizes or avoiding certain food groups might do more harm than good. Consulting a nutritionist can provide personalized advice based on your unique needs.

10.3. Essential Nutrients and their Sources

Postpartum nutritional requirements are elevated. So, let's delve into some essential nutrients crucial for every new mother.

- Iron: It's significant for hemoglobin formation and prevention of anemia. Iron-rich foods include leafy greens, meat, poultry, and dried fruit.
- Calcium: With breastfeeding occupying a central part of your routine, your calcium needs are high. Milk, yogurt, cheese, and fortified non-dairy milk are rich calcium sources.
- Vitamins A and C: These vitamins are instrumental for repairing tissues after childbirth. Find Vitamin A in carrots, sweet potatoes, and leafy green vegetables, while Vitamin C is abundant in citrus fruits, strawberries, and bell peppers.
- Omega-3 fatty acids: Renowned for their positive effects on brain

function and heart health. Seafood, flaxseed, chia seeds, and walnuts are examples of Omega-3 rich foods.

Remember, this is not an exhaustive list, and dietary needs may depend on individual health conditions and dietary preferences.

10.4. Nourishing Your Mind: Foods that Enhance Mood

A nutrient-rich diet can work wonders on your morale, helping to elevate mood and emotional wellbeing. Include these mood-lifting foods in your diet:

- Berries are rich in antioxidants that combat oxidative stress.
- Spinach boasts a high content of folate, which aids serotonin production.
- Nuts, particularly walnuts and almonds, contain proteins that help stabilize blood sugar levels, keeping mood swings in check.
- Dark Chocolate can increase serotonin levels, boosting mood and easing stress.
- Salmon is high in Omega-3 fatty acids, which are beneficial for brain health and mood enhancement.

10.5. Maiden Voyage into Mindful Eating

Paying attention to 'how' you eat is just as important as 'what' you eat. Mindful eating — the practice of savoring your meals by being fully present — can vastly improve not only your overall eating habits but also positively influence your mind, reducing stress and anxiety.

- Practice Gratitude: Before you begin your meal, take a moment to express gratitude for the nourishment the food provides. This simple act can bring about a sense of calm.
- Chew Thoroughly: Not just good for digestion. Chewing food slowly and thoroughly can help you enjoy the flavors, textures, and subtly enhance your eating experience.
- Avoid Distractions: Try to keep digital screens at bay during meal times. This can help you to better engage with your meal and eat just the right amount.

The eater's state of mind directly impacts digestion, and a calm, peaceful state can enable more efficient digestion and nutrient absorption.

10.6. Meeting Your Nutritional Needs: A Sample Meal Plan

It's important to strike a balance in your meals, making sure all your nutritional requirements are met. Below is a sample meal plan to take inspiration from:

Meal	Food	Nutrient
Breakfast	Whole grain oatmeal with mixed berries and a sprinkle of chia seeds	Complex Carbs, Vitamins, Omega-3
Mid-morning Snack	Almonds	Protein, Healthy Fats

Lunch	Seared salmon, Quinoa, Steamed vegetables	Omega-3, Protein, Fiber
Afternoon Snack	Yogurt topped with a banana	Protein, Calcium, Carbs
Dinner	Grilled chicken breast, Sweet potato mash, Spinach salad	Protein, Vitamins, Iron, Complex Carbs

Note: The above meal plan is a general guide and may not suit every individual. Always consult a nutritionist or healthcare provider for personalized dietary advice.

Nutrition is one giant step towards overall self-care. With a balanced diet, not only are you fueling your body healthily, but also giving your mind a much-needed nudge towards positivity and wellness. Remember, this journey of nourishment is as much about you as it is about your little one. Embrace the mantra of "Happy Mom, Healthy Baby."

Chapter 11. Seeking Professional Help: When and Why

The journey through motherhood can be likened to a rollercoaster, teeming with highs that take your breath away, and plunges that can stir anxiety. In this tumultuous ride, there may come a point when professional help becomes indispensable. It doesn't signify weakness or defeat, but rather a courageous step towards ensuring your wellness and the wellbeing of your child.

11.1. Identifying the Need

Firstly, it is crucial to recognize when professional help is needed. Often, mental health issues can be cloaked in seemingly ordinary 'baby blues,' which are common post-childbirth due to the surge and ebb of hormonal levels.

Symptoms of 'baby blues' such as mood swings, weepiness, or feelings of overwhelm, although common and usually short-lived, shouldn't be disregarded outright. While they can dissipate typically within a couple of weeks postpartum, if these signs persist or intensify, it could point towards more severe conditions like postpartum depression (PPD) or anxiety.

Other symptoms can include relentless sadness, severe mood swings, overpowering fatigue, intense irritability, difficulty bonding with the baby, withdrawal from friends or family, fear of not being a competent mother, feelings of worthlessness or inadequacy, or even thoughts of self-harm or harming the baby. These are immediate signs that professional intervention is needed.

Moreover, mental health issues might not always appear

immediately after the birth of the child. They can manifest later down the line, even many months post-delivery. This is recognized as late-onset PPD, and it's important to be vigilant about such changes, irrespective of the elapsed time since childbirth.

11.2. Exploring the Options

Once you've identified the need for professional help, the subsequent step is to explore the various types of professional services available. This can range from psychiatrists who can manage medication plans to psychologists or therapists who provide talk therapy.

Support groups can also be beneficial, where you can interact with other mothers who are experiencing similar challenges. Hearing their stories and solutions can provide perspective and make you feel less alone in your journey.

Furthermore, consider seeking help from a postpartum doula who can offer education and non-judgmental support, guide you in newborn care, and also provide physical aid around the house, giving you some much-needed respite and self-care time.

11.3. Choosing the Right Professional

Choosing the right mental health professional for your needs is integral to your recovery journey. This decision can depend upon multiple factors, such as their expertise, the severity of your symptoms, your comfort level with them, and your general preferences.

You might feel more at ease with a female professional, for instance, as there will be discussions about sensitive topics like breastfeeding or body changes. Or perhaps, you may prefer a professional who specializes in cognitive behavior therapy (CBT) if you find that approach helps you manage your symptoms more effectively. Trust your instincts, do your research, ask for recommendations, and decide what feels comfortable to you.

11.4. Preparing for the First Session

Once the therapist or professional has been chosen, prep for your first session. It can feel daunting, but remember, they are there to help and support you.

You might want to make a list of your symptoms, how they are affecting your daily life, any questions or concerns you have about therapy, and what you hope to achieve from it. This can give you a starting point in your discussions.

Pen down any significant life changes or stressful events that might be contributing to your feelings, even if they seem unrelated to motherhood. They will help the professional understand your situation better and design a suitable treatment plan.

11.5. Embracing the Process

Even with professional help, remember that recovery takes time and patience. You might have good days and bad, but every step forward, no matter how small, is a victory. Converse openly with your therapist, be honest about your feelings, and don't hesitate to speak up if something doesn't feel right about your treatment. Your therapist wants to help and will be willing to adjust the treatment plan to better suit you.

11.6. Remember, You're Not Alone

While professional help is necessary and advisable in certain situations, remember that you're not alone in this journey. Realize that seeking such help is not a sign of weakness, but an act of strength and self-love. So, take that step, reach out, and remember: this too shall pass, and you're doing a great job.

In conclusion, the journey of motherhood, although demanding and sometimes grueling, can be made smoother and more manageable with prompt recognition of the need for help and the right professional support. Above all, it's crucial to remember that seeking help is not only okay but sometimes necessary, for the wellbeing of both the mother and the child. After all, a well-nurtured, happy mother raises a well-nurtured, happy child.

Printed in Great Britain
by Amazon